I0404434

Ask the Coach

By John G. Agno, Certified Executive & Business Coach

Copyright 2012 Signature, Inc.

ISBN-10: 1481034960

ISBN-13: 978-1481034968

All Rights Reserved

This book may not be reproduced in any form without permission of the author. However, permission is granted to people who have purchased this publication and wish to reproduce the content of the book or select pages for their own personal use.

Readers should be aware that Internet websites offered as citations and/or sources for further information or book purchase may change or disappear between the times of writing and when read.

Limited of Liability/Disclaimer of Warranty: While the author has used his best efforts in preparing this book, he makes no representations or warranties with respect to the accuracy or completeness of the contents and specifically disclaims any implied warranties or merchantability or fitness for a particular purpose. No warranty may be created or extended by booksellers or sales representatives or written sales materials. The advice and strategies contained herein may not be suitable for your situation. You should consult with a professional where appropriate. The author shall be not be held liable for any loss of profit or any other personal or commercial damages, including but not limited to special, incidental, consequential, or other damages.

Table of Contents

What is Coaching?

The Art of Marketing

The Marketing Blind Spot

Seven Principles of Marketing:

1: Wash Your Hands of Wrong Assumptions

2: Achieve Staying Power

3: Expect the Unexpected

4: Use Your Technical & Marketing Strengths

5: Develop a Marketing Presence

6: High Gross Profit Sales…Always

7: Selling Someone Once Doesn't Make Them a Loyal Customer

Ask the Coach:

Doing What You Do Best

Providing Performance Feedback

Product versus Service Revenue Shift

What is Selling?

Selling More Products and Services

Freshen Up

How to Increase Your Sales

I'm Not Happy at Work

Working from Home Tips

Keeping Up With Client Demands

Starting Over

Encore Careers

How to Improve Chances for Moving Up the Corporate Ladder

Holiday Gifts

New Year Resolutions

Transformational Leadership

How to Keep Good Employees

Difficult Time Finding Talent

Dependable Part-Time Employees

How to Engage Employees

Developing a Winning Attitude

About the Author

What is Coaching?

Coaching is partnering with clients in a thought-provoking and creative process that inspires them to maximize their personal and professional potential. The coaching relationship is a strong, resilient, dependable and safe vehicle in which change can take place for the person being coached.

Professional coaches provide an ongoing partnership designed to help clients produce fulfilling results in their personal and professional lives. Coaches help people improve their performances and enhance the quality of their lives.

A coach is not a problem solver, teacher, advisor, instructor or expert. A coach is a listener, sounding board and awareness-raiser. Coaches are trained to listen, to observe and to customize their approach to individual client needs. They seek to elicit solutions and strategies from the client; they believe the client is naturally creative and resourceful. The coach's job is to provide support to enhance the skills, resources, and creativity that the client already has.

So what is professional coaching and how does it differ from consulting?

Download and listen to this MP3 recording of an interview of Coach John Agno at: http://view.vzaar.com/845767/download for the answer to that question.

All areas of coaching are most often characterized by one-to-one interactions that often are provided through face-to-face or telephone conversations. **These interactions**

share three essential core *competencies*: connection, clarification and commitment.

The core competencies are intertwined with one another in a continuous cycle of exploration and discovery of the espoused theory (what they say) and the theory in use (what they are observed doing) of the person being coached. The lack of integrity or coherence between these two theories is fertile ground for coaching interactions. In this way, the core competencies become the primary tool to surface and explore the discrepancy between the espoused theory and the theory in use. In addition, the competencies enhance the emotional intelligence of the person being coached, promoting personal, interpersonal and organizational effectiveness.

Each coaching session typically is result or goal-directed with emphasis on the person being coached taking action and sustaining changes over time. This action often is to improve performance in a specific area of interest to the person being coached and his or her employer, family and friends.

How does Coaching differ from Therapy?

Therapy is usually problem or crisis centered with emphasis on diagnosis, analysis, or healing. Therapy might include testing, prescribed drugs, and a focus on early life experiences, involvement of other family members and is typically grounded in theory.

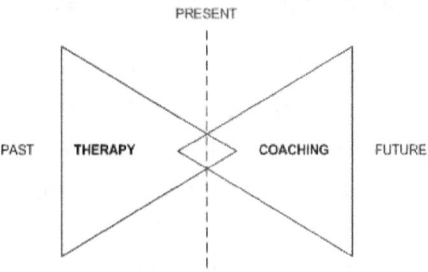

Using Time Perspective to Differentiate Coaching & Therapy Interactions

© Copyright 1997-2002 Mike R. Jay All Rights Reserved. This diagram may not be used, transmitted, stored or duplicated without expressed written permission of the author: www.b-coach.com

How does Coaching differ from Mentoring?

Mentoring can occur naturally, informally or formally. It can be part of a formal program with a mutually agreed upon contract for meetings or other arrangements or it can last a lifetime.

Mentoring most often includes an exchange of wisdom, support, learning or guidance for the purpose of personal, spiritual, and career or life growth. In the workplace, mentoring is sometimes used to achieve strategic business goals, such as retaining new employees and/or leadership succession planning. For example, a mentor could be a highly visible and experienced company executive advising a rising star. Unlike mentors, a coach can be less visible but very much present. Coaches are drawn from the outside to provide individual executive support on personal and business matters.

With so much structural change happening within the world economy, people recognize that they have many questions that demand answers. The purpose of this book is to illustrate some of those questions along with responds by a personal business coach.

The insights in this book are meant to help you develop the leadership skills necessary to become the master of yourself so you will be ready, willing and able to lead others. Self leadership happens through <u>self-learning</u> and self-coaching. As you build your capability to lead, people become attracted to you and this opens the door for trusting you. When they trust you, people will be open to listening to what you have to say.

The content in this book is based on self-coaching insights previously published in **The Ann Arbor Area Business Monthly** at: http://www.annarborbusinessmagazine.com and **The Entrepreneur Network at:** http://www.TENonline.org

The Art of Marketing

The "art" of marketing can be very mysterious to engineers, accountants, computer specialists, and other technically-oriented people. This is especially true when it comes to the commercialization of a new product or process or the startup of a technically-driven business venture.

Many technically-oriented people think that the key to marketing success is to learn the secret marketing "formulas." They take all the marketing courses at their local business school. They read all the books on marketing. But it still doesn't happen. The "formulas" aren't there.

In fact, they aren't anywhere. Marketing is much more an "art" than a science. It's simply a mistake to look for scientific formulas in a field of "art".

Successful commercialization combines the "science" of formulating a winning physical product/process with the "art" of marketing strategy and implementation. In a way, this combination of product science and marketing art emulates the craftsmen of yesteryear who applied crude tools with a system of methods and principles into a skillful performance that could not be learned solely by study.

In today's high-tech world, most technically-oriented product developers would be well advised to seek out a marketing artist to work with — rather than trying to become the all-in-one craftsman.

The development of xerography is a good example of the combination of product science and marketing art. Chester Carlson, a physicist and patent attorney, obtained a patent on xerography and searched for a way to commercialize it. He happened to be an attorney for a client of Battelle (a research organization in Columbus, OH), and sent a copy of the patent to them for review.

Battelle was interested. For 55% of the patent rights, Battelle agreed to invest in the technology, with Battelle research making three technical improvements. However, it was the little Haloid Company (a market-oriented 100-employee company in Rochester, NY) that figured out how to commercialize this expensive and very-service-intensive machine ($15,000 cost). As a result, in 1963 the Xerox 914 was born.

Joe Wilson, Haloid Company's president, is given the credit for the marketing "art" that led to the success of xerography — *Lease the Xerox 914 copier for only $100 a month, but pay an additional penny per copy made on the machine.*

It was Haloid's addition of marketing "art" to Battelle's solid product "science" that created a winning product. The marketing-oriented

Haloid Company changed its name to Xerox Corporation, and the technically-oriented Battelle received $350 million of Xerox stock.

Don't underestimate the need for marketing "art" in your own product or business development activities. Find a good marketing "artist" to work with — and do so as early as possible.

The Marketing Blind Spot

After working with hi-tech entrepreneurs for several years now, one major failing keeps surfacing -- too many have a fatal marketing "blind spot".

These entrepreneurs thoroughly understand their technology. They may well be on their way to mastering the engineering and operational issues involved in delivering their product or service. Yet they persist -- often until it is too late -- in believing that the marketing issues are relatively simple -- *because everyone will surely love their new product or service as much as they do*.

Only after that product or service is "ready" -- or worse, after early sales attempts have bombed -- will someone like me get a call. Of course, at that point most of the money's gone. Sometimes huge amounts! There's neither time nor money to do a competent marketing plan, let alone execute it -- and the venture fails -- needlessly.

In my experience, this marketing "blind spot" is the single most common cause of hi-tech startup failures -- in fact, I'm starting to believe, more common than all others combined.

The most important piece of advice that I can give hi-tech entrepreneurs -- and it's probably not limited to hi-tech -- is to get a marketing "reality check" early on -- like at the beginning, before you even know that your technology will do what you're hoping it will do.

Hire an independent objective professional to take a look at your intended market. Is it really there? Can it be penetrated (or developed) by a startup and what's likely to be required to do so? This is just a "look". It doesn't have to be an expensive, complicated project. In fact, at this point, it shouldn't be. But it's absolutely certain that it will be much less "expensive" than if it's done downstream.

Seven Principles of Marketing

Principle #1: Wash Your Hands of Wrong Assumptions — To Keep Your Business From Slipping Down The Drain

The way we think is conditioned by our life experiences. If we've spent our life in a classroom, we tend to think as a student or teacher. If we've spent our work life as an employee, we tend to think as an employee.

Many new entrepreneurs talk-the-talk of the entrepreneur — but their thinking is still grounded in their life as an employee. This can be deadly to their goals and aspirations.

Most employees don't think about where the money comes from to pay their weekly wages and benefits. Or how the cash must flow to meet next month's payroll. Or what accounts are becoming payable, or when tax deposits, rent, and loan payments are due. Or where the money will come from to allow the company to deliver a large order just received from its largest customer...

It's difficult for an employee to learn to think "outside the box" — whereas the entrepreneur thinks only outside the box, because the box is the venture, and the entrepreneur needs to keep the box firm, clean, full and together.

New entrepreneurs must learn to continually question their assumptions. The decisions that are most likely to come back and bite them — perhaps put them out of business — are typically NOT the consequence of bad judgment or faulty reasoning — *but the consequence of applying perfectly sound judgment to wrong assumptions.*

The following are a few all-too-common "wrong assumptions."

- **Everyone will love my product/service as much as I do.**
  They will NOT! Period. They will not see ANY of the advantages and benefits you see — until you make them stop and recognize and think about them — each and every one. That's called selling — and that requires a great deal of time and energy, and more than a little money — if only to keep food on the table during that time — which you can safely figure is going to be 10 times longer than your most

conservative estimate.

- **A good product/service will sell itself.** ...or... **If I build it, they will come and buy it**.
  Don't let these assumptions trick you into spending most of your resources in "getting ready". At least as much — and probably more — will be required after you are ready. Get that "reality check" early. Get out and talk to customers — not friends, neighbors, or even end users, but the people that you're going to be selling to — distributors, retailers, purchasing agents, etc. — before you spend ANY resource — and then keep talking to them — through development, through test, through manufacture, through delivery — and after.

- **In this business, I must purchase (build, own, have, rent, show, etc.) _____.**

  Not if you can't afford them! And affordability isn't limited to just not having the money. If such acquisitions would seriously reduce your margin for errors, if they would decimate your life savings, or expose you to impossible debt, or put you into business with investors you neither know nor understand — you'd better stop and think hard about whether they really are "affordable". If you decide they're not affordable, that doesn't mean you have to give up. It just means you have to look for "better ways" — ways to do what you want to do with what you CAN afford. And in the process, you just may discover that the new ways you find — albeit through necessity — result in better value — including quality, service and/or price — to your customers.

- **My competitors have _____; therefore I must also.** Your customers are looking to buy the best VALUE — from either you or your competitors. If you simply copy your competitors, where's your edge — where's your added value? Going in, your competitors have all the advantages. They're better established. They have more capital, more resources, more contacts, more knowledge... You need an edge. And you find that edge by looking for things they're doing — preferably things that cost them considerable capital or operational resources — that you can "invent" ways of doing as well or better for less.

- **My customers expect me to have _____.**

    Your customers expect you to own a factory? To have an expensive office? To entertain them lavishly? Don't believe it! Excellence in delivery — in quality, service, and price — will overcome these "handicaps" every time. Yes, you may have to sell a little harder without the expected trappings to buttress your selling, but it's not impossible, nor even particularly difficult — and it beats either of the alternatives of doing nothing or going broke.

- **My business plan is so good, it just can't fail**.

Danger! Great business plans fail every day. Things never happen the way they're planned. Sales will not grow as quickly as you project, costs will be significantly higher, times will be significantly longer... Think of your business plan as a *compass* — not as a *road map*. Let it point the way — but don't let it blind you to the "unexpected". Your success — or failure — will largely be determined by how well you see and handle the unexpected.

- **It's important that I not make mistakes**.
  Wrong! It's important that you not *persist* in mistakes — that you recognize your mistakes early and "correct" them (i.e., try a different approach) before they get out of hand and become *costly* mistakes.

You're going to make mistakes. In fact, you *want* to make mistakes. You learn from your mistakes — not from your successes. If you're not making mistakes, you're suffering "opportunity loss" — which can be just as detrimental to your business as any operational loss.

These are just a few examples of assumptions that can — and have — derailed otherwise viable businesses. Every decision we make is based on assumptions — most of which we're not even aware of until we stop and think them through. The way to minimize bad business decisions is to minimize bad business assumptions. And the best way to minimize bad assumptions is to stay constantly aware of how susceptible we all are to them.

Principle #2: Achieve Staying Power by Remaining Flexible

To meet the challenges of survival, an entrepreneur must understand and follow certain rules of competition — in addition to having a good idea and a market that has at least a marginal interest in that idea.

Each challenge comes with its own pressures — but failure to respond to these challenges with flexibility can — and all too often does — lead directly to the venture's demise.

The following are a few important "rules of competition". Break them at your peril! Following these rules will keep your venture flexible — and greatly enhance its prospects for survival.

- *Compete on a "variable" versus a "fixed" cost basis.*
  Because there are virtually no economies of scale for small businesses, there is little reason to invest in capital equipment that brings down your costs of goods sold in volume production. The less fixed costs you have to support, the more survivable your business will be when facing the unexpected. Always — your first choice should be to outsource versus investing in bricks or paychecks!

- *Conserve cash by managing cash flow.*
  Control costs by fostering a frugal corporate culture — through your example. Lavish perks send the wrong message to both employees and customers. Strive to get paid early by customers, pay

suppliers late, and pay yourself last. Don't expect to pay yourself a salary until you are absolutely certain that the business venture has consistent sustaining monthly revenues. Having a positive cash flow is a key element in ensuring that you have the flexibility to react to business changes.

- *Continually adjust your product/service to the market.* Your product/service should be unique enough to differentiate your venture from your competitors — but not so different that customers don't know what to make of it. Listen to your customers! Involve them when changing your product or service — to guard against isolation and arrogance. Accept change in the marketplace by striving to obsolete your own products and services — before your rivals figure out how to do it themselves.

- *Invest only in technology that increases business flexibility.* The use of advanced telecommunications — as an infrastructure for reengineering business processes — may provide you with better time management (read: productivity) and thus competitive advantage. For example, if you or your employees are mostly with your customers (i.e., out of the office), a notebook computer for anywhere-database decision making, report/proposal writing, and/or eMail communication with associates could increase your responsiveness to customer requests.

- *Use a mentor or consultant to help guide you through the reengineering of business processes.*
Doing things differently can allow your venture to make a quantum leap over the competition — or cause you to crash land the venture. It is always important to talk through your planned actions with someone who has an arms-length relationship with the venture, who has good business judgement, and who will be open with you and your blind spots. The market place will continually push you to rethink your strategies. You need to bounce your new ideas off someone who will treat your discussions seriously.

Principle #3: Expect the Unexpected

Unexpected events — surprises, whether good or bad — can make or break your business. Your ability to recognize and react to these events is key to both your growth — and your survival. As an entrepreneur, you must have enough *knowledge* to plan and anticipate, yet enough *street saavy* to know when things are going unusually right or unusually wrong.

We're talking here about really big surprises — like discovering that one of your products is selling much better than expected — and you don't know why ...or... discovering that you are selling to the wrong customers ...or... that your product or service needs to be revamped from top to bottom ...or... even discovering you are in the wrong business.

For example, you may have started your company to be in the software *product* business, but month after month your computer consulting *service* revenue far outpaces your software sales. This is a good clue that you should begin to rethink your business strategy.

You may not need to switch businesses, but, clearly, you should change your resource allocation and operations management in recognition that the company is now consulting-services driven. With this altered strategy, your software development efforts might better be redirected toward providing a stronger competitive edge for securing and maintaining your consulting-service customers.

The Chinese word for crisis is "wei ji". When written, the calligraphic representation is the combination of two words: "peril" and "opportunity". Management of the unexpected is to understand the perils of the current situation while, at the same time, having the vision to seize the opportunities presented.

Your acceptance that your marketplace is in constant flux is key to your understanding that the marketplace will unexpectedly push you to rethink your business strategy —--- hopefully before your competition rethinks their strategy!

Principle #4: Use Your Technical & Marketing Strengths

It's always difficult to see the frame when you're part of the picture.

However, it's vital that entrepreneurs make the effort to determine and clearly understand their technical and marketing strengths relative to their competitors — and then to take best advantage of those strengths to differentiate themselves from those competitors.

Customers' buying decisions are based upon their **perception** of the **best value** available — from your company or your competitors.

Note that "best value" does not necessarily mean lowest cost. Value is composed of service, quality and price. Only after doing everything possible to deliver exceptional service and quality, should entrepreneurs even think of competing on price-- more about that in Principle #6.

Note also that it is "perceived" value that counts. Perception is how others view you. You have a great deal of control over that — not only by what and how you deliver — but also by how you present yourself — in person, in your letters, in your literature, in your advertising.

If you clearly understand your technical and marketing strengths, you can deliver a consistent and powerful message. If you don't, you can't. Recognize that nobody will know why they should buy from you until you tell them. However, if you tell them you're great at "everything", that's simply hype, and nobody will believe you.

If your company is small and your competitors are large, you should generally engage in "guerilla marketing" against their "conventional marketing". Try to promote your small company's speed and mobility against their superior resources.

Pit your "flexibility" against their "standard practices", your "privacy" against their "public disclosures", your synergistic "strategic alliances" against their inclination to "go it alone", your "buy" (read: outside subcontracting) against their "make" (read: internal production), your "cherry picking" of high margin business to their tendency to "do it all".

For example, a large competitor with a labor-intensive assembly operation (with growing fringe benefit costs and escalating labor rates) can be a wonderful target for a small innovative company (with little investment in production facilities or sales channels) that can take advantage of short product life cycles to lead the market.

To understand your strategic technical and marketing strengths, analyze what your customers want to buy compared to what your competitors can't readily deliver. And then structure your organization, your operations — and your "image" — around those strengths.

Principle #5: Develop a Marketing Presence

To survive and prosper, a small company must establish a *marketing presence* based upon a *sustainable competitive advantage*.

Let's begin to explore this principle (which makes it easy for people to buy from you) by first defining some terms:

- *Marketing presence* is the message your business communicates to its prospect and customer base. To be effective, the message should be clear and simple — and contain the key attributes you want associated with your business.

- *Competitive advantage* is the sum of those attributes that differentiate your business from its competitors. This is your *core competence*. You develop, build and enhance it through a clear understanding of your customers' wants and needs. You implement it through a strategic plan (a directional compass) that can help you quickly adapt to changes in their wants and needs.

- *Sustainable* means to keep in existence, to maintain and affirm the validity of, to support the spirit, vitality and resolution of, to encourage, to endure/withstand. Only through your continuous understanding of what makes your business competitive can your business survive and prosper. GE's former CEO, Jack Welch, once said, "If you don't have a competitive advantage, don't compete."

Since it takes two — a buyer and a seller — to make a sale, the reason for establishing a viable marketing presence is for your business to be on the prospective buyer's "short list" when the buyer is ready to buy. You want to be sure that your company is among those being evaluated when the prospect's need arises.

When you think about your competitive advantage, consider that in your prospect's mind your company "fits" into some category.

For example, you are either a "low-cost" or "value-added" supplier. A low-cost supplier is categorized as one who consistently provides a lower cost with acceptable quality. A value-added supplier provides a differentiated product or service that contains substantial attributes which command a premium price.

Likewise, you are either a "generalist" or a "specialist". A generalist is categorized as having a broad scope — serving all types of customers in an industry or geographical area, offering a broad range of products or services. A specialist focuses on specific products or services and dedicates all efforts to that one niche or market segment.

The key element in your thinking should be to make a difference. You must take the risk to create a recognizable choice from your rival companies. Your worst error here would be trying to imitate rival companies or trying to be all things to all people.

As you think strategically about establishing your market presence, consider this process:

- *Conceptualize your strategy —* this is pure and analytical.

- *Engineer general agreement to the strategy —* here you are muddling over the practicality of what you want to do and sharing your ideas with others and getting their input.

- *Prepare a mission statement and business plan —* to discover and clarify what business you are in and how you plan to approach it.

- *Communicate the statement and plan* — both internally and externally.

- *Live the plan* — if all the steps feel right, start to implement the plan —— but with the full expectation, knowledge and intent that you will continuously adjust and adapt it to market changes.

Principle #6: High Gross Profit Sales...Always

Years ago, I began printing basic pricing and inventory formulas on the back of my calling card because most people I met did not know how to set a selling price based on their cost of merchandise — or, conversely, how to arrive at an acceptable cost of merchandise when they knew the price point at which the item should be sold.

Or how to calculate important indicators like Markup Percentage, Turnover, Inventory Return on Investment, Percentage Return on Inventory, etc. Successful businesses strive constantly to do more with less — and the use of such indicators to actively manage product pricing, inventory turns, people productivity, etc., is a very important part of their success.

Pricing has an immediate impact on your business — positive or negative. That's why it's strategically important. Unfortunately, common sense pricing is not always common in practice — due sometimes to lack of knowledge of how to set prices, but much more frequently simply to bad assumptions based on the unquestioned acceptance of prevailing myths and rules-of-thumb. Pricing determines the profit of your business both *directly* — as the result of revenues less costs — and *indirectly* — in its influence on stakeholder (customer, vendor, employee, investor, etc.) perceptions.

Let's look at three common myths that tempt entrepreneurs to lower their pricing — tending to lead inexorably to their ultimate business failure:

- **Myth #1: Low-Price Leadership is Sustainable.**

    For a small business, *there are no economies of scale* — and, therefore, low-price leadership is *not* sustainable. Wal-Mart and K-Mart can operate on 18 to 20% mark-ups because of their large turnover — but your business can't. If you believe your customers' loyalty is to price alone, you are destined to wind up in a "How long can we go and still add margin dollars?" battle with your competitors. If your competitors are larger — or better financed — or better connected — the odds are overwhelming that you'll lose.

In making volume pricing decisions, be *very* careful of over-reliance on your cost details. Most entrepreneurs' cost details represent best estimates (including cost reduction ideas) — and exclude the extraordinary (never to happen again) mistakes that caused overtime and material waste on the last order. Be assured that the highest percentage of credit problems, schedule changes and other cost impairments will come from your discounted high volume deals.

- **Myth #2: The Market Knows the Value of Your Product.**

    Salespeople do what they are trained to do. Their job is to close orders — to bring in revenue. When they are sitting in front of a customer and are asked to lower the price, they decide who is easier to sell — you or the customer. If you haven't given them firm pricing rules — and adhere to them — don't be surprised when they decide the easier sell is you.

    High gross margin dollars are absolutely necessary to your small business — to pay the selling expenses of telling the market the value of your products and services. You *must* be willing to risk losing orders — regardless of their perceived importance — if they cannot be obtained at pricing that yields a real (not estimated) profit.

- **Myth #3: Lack of Profits is Normally Caused by High Costs.**

  It's easy to underestimate your operating and overhead costs in setting prices. And the cost most frequently underestimated is what it costs to sell the product or service — including everything from salaries for salespeople, to their travel expenses, to advertising, to shows and conferences, to distribution markups, etc. In a $3.50 box of cereal, for example, the highest costs are $.50 for advertising and coupons. The flakes are next at $.07. Almost all the rest is transportation and the manufacturer and distribution mark-ups.

Believing that lack of profits results only from high costs fails to recognize the importance of setting — and maintaining — adequate-margin pricing. Be sure to include *all* your costs in your prices. And if that requires pricing away some business, so be it. That's the business most likely to put you under.

Principle #7: Selling Someone Once Doesn't Make Them a Loyal Customer

Making the first sale to a customer is very expensive. It takes a lot of advertising and promotion dollars — and a lot of time, energy and money chasing dead ends — to land a customer. Yet subsequent sales to that customer are relatively inexpensive — and profitable. Too many businesses make the mistake of focusing on generating more sales to first-time buyers — rather than working harder to build sales with the customers they already have.

With first-time buyers, you not only have the costs of getting that first order, but you still have to *build* a foundation of mutual trust if you hope to get follow-on orders. With your existing customers, you've already built this foundation of trust — you only have to *maintain* it — by continuing to deliver quality products and service. Cultivating broad and deep relationships with your existing customers allows you to focus your limited resources wisely — building as great a share of their business as possible — while your competition fights tooth and nail just to get their foot in the door.

This customer-driven (versus product-driven or technology-driven) strategy goes by many names: Relationship Marketing, Retention Marketing, Frequency Marketing, Loyalty Marketing, Frequent Customer Marketing, etc. But whatever you choose to call it is not nearly as important as your understanding that *your existing customers offer your greatest profit potential*.

Here again the old "80/20 Rule" applies: In an established business, 80% of your sales come from 20% of your customers. These are the customers to focus on. If you don't know who they are — if you can't list them — in order of decreasing sales — find out. Analyze your sales and make a list — and hang that list where you can see it every day. And every day, ask yourself, "How can I build my sales with these customers? How can I strengthen my relationship with them?"

Here are some suggestions:

- Look for ways of maintaining an on-going flow of information with them. Think of them — and try to get them to think of you — as a "business partner". Personal phone calls... Visits... A customer advisory council... Etc.

- Make the effort to learn their business so thoroughly that you can initiate new areas of business activity between you and them that can profit both of you. If there's a product or service that's giving them grief — or from a vendor they're not totally comfortable with — try to figure out a way to provide that product or service yourself. Even if it's not a product or service you currently offer — or had planned to offer. Keep in mind that it's often easier and less costly to add new products/services than it is to add new customers.

- Add additional services — preferably unique to your customer's needs — that demonstrates your attention to the small but important details — and helps keep your competitor's foot out of the door.

- Think about adding "loyalty" programs where you can reward your customers' loyalty in ways that your competitors can't easily copy.

The evolution of a customer-driven business begins with your understanding of how important it is to invest your time and resources to be in constant communication with this 20% of your customer base. Cultivating relationships and making these customers more successful is not just a salesman's job. It's much smarter to get someone else to stay in the office and run your operations so you (the entrepreneur) can be out helping your key customers take care of their business!

Ask the Coach: Doing What You Do Best.

Q: I just returned from vacation where I had a chance to think about how I want to live my life differently. I know that I want do something else in my career but I am not sure what. Do you have any advice on what I can do about this discontent that I am feeling?

A: Every year, we gain a clearer understanding that without positive change, decline is inevitable. Still it's easy to lose hope: barriers to change seem to be everywhere. We work in organizations that aren't much fun. We fail to gain work/life balance that is so important to us but so difficult to sustain. Looking ahead, the challenge is to recognize that what we are now tolerating can be reinvented.

Most people returning to work from a relaxing vacation, where they took stock of their life, question if they are on the right career path but don't do anything about it. "I'll be happy when...." is the way many people think they are living their lives. A fortunate few decide not to languish in their present job and begin the process of engineering a mid-career correction. Here is how these very few do it.

They recognize that happiness is not something that happens to you. Happiness is inside you now. You are motivated from within as you discovered while on vacation. You only have to allow happiness to continue to surface after the vacation in your work and personal lives.

<u>The formula for happiness</u> is to know yourself, discover what you do best and understand that you get what you tolerate. In medicine, you look at how "well tolerated" a drug will be related to its side effects. At work and at home, many people evaluate new opportunities related to what can be well tolerated. Yet after life, most people don't want their tombstone to read, "She tolerated stuff for other people because they paid her." Especially, when we realize that we can make more money and have more fun doing work that engages our passions. Life is too short for doing work you don't enjoy.

That said, I don't recommend that you immediately leave your job but do begin the career transition process to visualize where you want to be. The first step is to change the way you think about yourself. Since what we think, we become, it is important to convince ourselves that we can change, so we do change. Believing comes first, then change, not the other way around. This rethinking who we are helps us to begin to consciously separate ourselves from our current job and life.

As you become clearer on where you want to be, you begin to modify your career path to be more in line with who you have become. Clarity happens as you get to know more about who you are by engaging in self-learning exercises. You also speed up the career transformation process through taking some self-assessments to match your strengths, interests and personality with potential work choices.

Everyone should know the important things in their life---your family, your partner, your health and well-being, your children---anything that is so important to you that if it were lost, you would be devastated.

After you know what's important to you, engage in selective reading and take a few personality and career self assessments to get to know you better. Here are some self-assessments in books that you can buy at your local or
online bookseller:

 Tom Rath: StrengthsFinder 2.0

 Marcus Buckingham: StandOut: The Groundbreaking New Strengths Assessment from the Leader of the Strengths Revolution

Kevin W. McCarthy: The On-Purpose Business: Doing More of What You Do Best More Profitably

The results of practicing the new discoveries and habits you learn over time are that they become part of your new real self.

Often, with changes in your habits, come changes in your aspirations and dreams. Going through the discovery of uncovering an ideal vision of yourself motivates you to develop new abilities to create and sustain the new habits. That is, you see the person you want to be---living with the new habit. This becomes the source of the energy required to work at the difficult and often frustrating process of change.

Ask the Coach: <u>Providing Performance Feedback</u>

Q: My question is how to deal with, from a management perspective, the issue of tardiness and absenteeism? I have to admit that this issue continues to be emotionally draining for me affecting both my attitude and that of those around me.

A: Many employers struggle with providing performance feedback to correct workplace issues, like tardiness and absenteeism.

What's performance feedback all about? The word "performance" makes it seem as if we are on stage. Success at work is our applause, the managers and leaders of our organization are the directors and producers, and our successful performance run is obviously the bottom line. Very few actors walk away with a Tony or an Oscar for mediocre performances. That is also true in the work world. Survival as an organization rests on the quality of our work. Without stopping to playback our performance, we might find that our run will be much shorter than we anticipated.

As leaders, we need to get people on a positive course by helping them face and then manage weaknesses. How this is done is through the feedback process: honestly, respectfully, openly, thoughtfully and with a sense of purpose.

For example, as a team leader or manager you can begin to work on the tardiness and absenteeism situation by writing out your answers to the following two questions:

1. How can you say that you are concerned about this weakness in a respectful and helpful way? (Be specific. "You aren't contributing to the team's effort" is a difficult statement for someone to hear. Reformat the weakness. "I am concerned when you don't get to the office on time" refocuses the concern as a problem.)
2. How can you offer this person encouragement to change the way he or she has done things in the past?

Employees want to succeed in their work. Most accept that goal-directed feedback is an effective means of guiding their work activities to be in concert with team and organizational goals. By having a performance feedback conversation with the tardy employee (<u>where you coach</u> while doing more listening than talking), you can insist that he arrive on time, focus on his work and ask what he will do to make this happen. The impact on the tardy employee will make him responsible for his actions and sets clear expectations. The consequence is he has the opportunity to design a solution to the issue.

This situation is an opportunity for you, as the team leader, to build your <u>leadership skills and style</u>. Leadership development is not an event. It is a process of participating in respectful conversations where the leader recognizes his or her own feelings and those of others in building safe and trusting relationships. Leadership is an interactive conversation that pulls people toward becoming comfortable with the language of personal responsibility and commitment.

COACH

Here are five guiding principles for respectful conversations:

1. When peers connect change happens. Effective coaching can happen on the dance floor of conversation.

2. It's okay to begin a conversation by confronting the other person with questions that seem awkward but set the stage for a respectful exchange. Why waste time on small talk? Just ask to-the-point information-seeking questions, like: "What are you here for? How do you want to spend our time together?"

3. Conversations are not meant to be structured. Be open to conversations that you are unprepared for and

focused on the interests of the other person (not your purpose).

4. Don't get pulled into solving problems that may not matter to the other person.
Allow time for the person to get to what's really important. Provide spaces where they can express their doubts and fears by being a thoughtful listener--without
taking on the responsibility to fix or debate the issue. After all, you have invited the person to talk about what matters to her or him, not you, so allow time for the articulation of those thoughts and feelings.

5. Personal transformation happens when the right questions get asked--not by providing answers. When you focus on the solution, you are trying to sell the person something. When you allow people to answer their own questions, they discover what they

were not aware of---and what is needed to move forward.

Ask the Coach: **Product versus Service Revenue Shift**

Q: Last year, we sold more professional services than expected. Now it looks like our services revenue will be higher than that generated from software product sales by the end of the year. What key success factors should we watch to maintain our company profits?

A: Managing professional services tends to be highly predictable with a steady positive cash flow. Whereas, managing a product business can result in very unpredictable swings in monthly revenue generation.

The fluctuation in revenue is one reason why product sales generally carry higher profit margins than the steady cash flow generated from service fees.

Set and monitor product and service line gross profit margins

Professional services have become a commodity in most industries and this has resulted in competitive pricing. So, I would suspect that your concern about maintaining gross profits of the past, when product sales dominated your business, is very real now that operations are more services oriented. When the majority of your revenue came from high margin product sales, you could afford to provide lower margin professional services to train new customers and implement product solutions. Now that services are exceeding product sales, your overall gross profit margins are, most likely, dropping.

Maintaining a profitable balance between services and product revenue can improve overall company profitability. Proprietary equipment or software sales allow for slightly higher margin services fees when the customer is locked into your product. Conversely, product-educated service providers can steer prospects toward buying your proprietary high margin products. Everyone sells what they know will work best for the customer.

Test business strategy by knowing what customers think of you.

If you think your business is now and will be more services-driven than product-driven, it is time to rethink your business and pricing strategy. Very large companies in the information technology industry, like IBM, are successfully moving from product-driven to services-driven businesses. Having your product customers outsource their management and maintenance services to your company may prove to be a long-term win-win arrangement.

Once you decide on what drives your business, services or products, it is time to check to see how your customers and potential customers see your company. Customers' buying decisions are based upon their perception of the best value available. Value is comprised of service, quality and price. Note that it's "perceived value" that counts.

Perception is how others view us. You have a great deal of control over that perception; in how you and your employees present your company in person, advertising, correspondence and brochures, and what you deliver in product or services. If you clearly understand your company's technical and marketing strengths relative your competitors, you can deliver a consistent and powerful message. A key success factor is to periodically test to see how your customers' perceptions have evolved---to always know what they really think about your firm.

Periodically analyze what your customers want to buy from you.

When you and your employees are delivering products or services to customers, you receive "grazing rights" within your customer's place of business. These grazing rights give you the ability to look for new opportunities where your firm can provide something that your competitors can't readily deliver.

Once you have defined what that new service or product might be, informally ask your customer contacts if they would be interested in buying such a product or service from you. If their answer is "yes," explore what it would take to structure your organization, your operations and your company's image around these new strengths.

Developing and delivering new customer-driven products and services can lead to consistently profitable revenue growth.

[John Agno: Can't Get Enough Leadership](#) (ebook formats at $2.99)

John G. Agno: Can't Get Enough Leadership: Self Coaching Secrets (Paperback at $28.99)

Ask the Coach: What is Selling?

Q: I am a small business owner and want to increase my sales revenue. What coaching tips might help me and my employees get better at selling?

A: Let's begin with a question or two: What is selling? Is it more than providing a well-defined product or service solution to an ill-defined problem?

Robert Louis Stevenson said, **_Everyone lives by selling something._** Yet most people don't understand the sales process and their part within it. Business owners constantly worry about the selling function and how it affects their ability to manage the firm's cash flow.

As a business coach, I don't sell "coaching" but do sell the results or benefits of engaging in a coaching relationship: improved business management, sales & marketing, planning, productivity/effectiveness and leadership. I do sell the value of brainstorming with, being accountable to, being listened to, receiving encouragement from someone who brings an independent viewpoint to the conversation.

Just like me, you have to come up with how you help your customers get better at what they do (or want to do) through satisfying customer wants and needs. When you do, you will know what selling is for your business.

 Once you know what selling is, the next question is, "How many people does it take to make a sale?"

This is not a trick question. It takes both a buyer and a seller to make a sale. That means the sales person can't make a sale without finding a prospect that may buy what is for sale. When the buyer is ready, willing and able to purchase what you sell, you want to be sure that your business is on the prospective customer's short list of places to shop. To do this you must first <u>establish a market presence</u> that is attractive to the prospective buyer.

The next question is, "Why do sales people fail?"

There are two main reasons why most sales people fail:

1. They think they can get away with "winging it."

This expression comes from the theater; where it alludes to an actor studying his part in the wings (the areas to either side of the stage) because he has been suddenly called on to replace another. First recorded in 1885, it eventually was extended to other kinds of improvisation based on unpreparedness.

Being prepared for the customer interaction is important. Knowing what action you want the prospect to take based upon this sales interaction allows the sales person to focus. Having a strategy of what to ask, what to show and tell helps to move the prospect to taking the desired action. Anticipating obstacles to the sale will allow you to plan how to go around or over potential "road-blocks" in accomplishing your sales objective.

2. They don't understand <u>the impact of their personality</u> on specific buying styles.

This shows up in not really listening to the prospective customer and, instead, filling the sales interaction with sales talk. They don't answer questions well because they don't listen for the assumptions/beliefs that's behind the prospect's words.

Their presentations are not in line with what the prospect wants to know. Being out-of-touch with the prospective customer's personality style insures that the inability to communicate will sour the sale.

Assessments

To improve your sales people's ability to sell well, train and coach them on a proven sales methodology that allows them to prepare for every major sales interaction. Provide them an understanding of their personality's strengths and weaknesses and how they can "read" their prospect's buying style. Usually a sales person's weakness, in the buyer's perspective, is an over extension of a strength and can be toned down through self-management by the sales person.

Knowing how to read people is dependent upon picking up on and interpreting hidden cues. Studies show that the brain processes four primary codes of communication. Two of these (speech and vocal codes) are processed auditorily, while the other two (facial expression and body language) are processed visually. When assessing people, we must interpret all four codes of communication — observing how they move, how they comport themselves, how they sound, and what they say.

The body language code (the combination of movement, gestures, and mannerisms) communicates a lot about people — such as: are they lying or telling the truth, do they like you, and do they actually mean what they are saying.

For example, people who lean in towards you are showing that they are interested in you and what you have to say. This is also the case if someone copies your body language (e.g. crossing legs in unison, clasping fingers, etc.). People who feel powerful and confident usually take up more physical space while people that stand too far away are being arrogant, snobby, or simply showing that they don't like you.

As you and your sales people improve your ability to read people, you will know much more about those you deal with and make better decisions on how to approach them.

Ask the Coach: Selling More Products and Services

Q: Can you provide any information on what small businesses are doing today to sell more product or services?

A: Too many businesses make the mistake of focusing on generating more sales to first-time buyers -- rather than working harder to build sales with the customers they already have. Making the first sale to a customer is very expensive. It takes a lot of advertising and promotion dollars--and a lot of time, energy and money chasing dead ends--to land a customer. Yet, subsequent sales to that customer are relatively inexpensive and very profitable.

Cultivating broad and deep relationships with your existing customers allows you to focus your limited resources wisely -- building as great a share of their business as possible -- while your competition fights tooth and nail just to get their foot in the door.

The Internet has become deeply embedded in our daily lives.

Today, most American households have Internet access. A blended marketing approach for your business can maintain a high frequency of touches and provide enough content to keep customers engaged. Most customers choose to engage with you online because they are increasingly reliant on the Internet. Your company's customized landing page provides a complete message but is slanted in favor of the topic most relevant to the arriving customer. The Internet has made it possible to reach out to an almost limitless market, at any time, and usually for little cost.

Anecdotal evidence shows that websites using both search engine optimization of organic listings and paid search strategies increase conversion rates because traffic goes up dramatically with links in multiple positions. Users choose to click more frequently on an organic listing when they also see a sponsored listing.

"The Role of Search in Consumer Buying," a study by comScore (sponsored by Google) found that 63 percent of search-related purchases occur in offline retail stores. The results also indicate that 25 percent of searchers purchased an item directly related to their search query—and of those buyers, just 37 percent completed their purchase online.

Blogs offer a personal touch on the Internet

There's also growing anecdotal evidence about the grassroots impact blogs can have on sales for companies, especially small businesses. Business owners are discovering the best way to keep customers happy and coming back is by directly communicating with them utilizing Weblogs or 'blogs' over the Internet.

Blogs humanize the Internet and keep you in touch with what's going on with customers. Blogging allows you to create an interactive customer conversation on subjects of mutual interest. People feel they can really have a conversation with someone who has a blog.

Communicating well doesn't have to drain your energy and creativity by spending extended hours engaging in community and regional meetings, telephone conferences or exchanging

many email messages.
Using blogging technology can allow you to connect with both colleagues and customers across the country to tell them what you are working on without having to be present.

Personally, I maintain four blogs to connect with present and future clients using a low-cost service provider. The Leadership Blog at www.coachingtip.com blog focuses on leadership tips, the www.sobabyboomer.com blog delivers life tips to the Baby Boomer Generation, the www.CareerWomenCoaching.com blog provides tips for career women and the www.Ask-Know-Do.com blog provides answers to frequently asked questions.

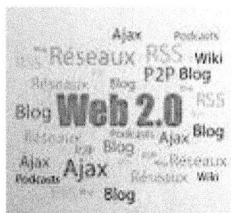 **Here are a few coaching tips for creating effective blogs:**

Focus on what is of interest your customers.

Set up your blog so each post gets its own permanent URL/permalink and heading.

Think of your blog as a database so your customers can search for content in past posts.

Blog frequently and regularly.

Use striking images in your posts to gain favorable attention.

Enable comments to interact with customers.

Ask the Coach: <u>Freshen Up</u>

Q: My business seems to be getting stale to our customers. What can I do to make it fresher?

A: Today, there are many alternative places to shop for goods and services. And there is much we don't understand about the nature of the value exchange between our business and its customers. Because different people value different things, we constantly work to understand what it takes to win each customer's business.

However, there are some things we do know. We know that it costs 8 to

10 times as much to attract a new customer as it does to keep a current customer. We know the average business loses 10% to 30% of their customers every year. The reason for this is customer satisfaction does not equal customer loyalty; of customers who defect, 80% are actually satisfied with the company's service. So, how does a business build customer loyalty?

Keeping the buying experience attractive can make all the difference

Using what you know about customers and practicing the "<u>law of attraction</u>," to appeal to both conscious and unconscious desires, is a good place to begin in making your business fresher and more appealing.

Customers are human. Every customer interaction is inherently unpredictable. Yet, every business needs to create a true dialog with its customer. As the customer relationship evolves over a series of interactions, the customer leaves many clues to guide the business in providing truly differentiated and personal attention.

In the business world, we don't speak much about the heart. Yet, our unique business purpose should come from the heart---since all businesses are ultimately people serving people. People need connection, belonging and meaningful contribution. Long after the product or service has been delivered, the feelings gained through the business interaction remain for the customer.

 Moments-in-time of every buying experience

The "moment-in-time" of every customer interaction is made up of three things: the experience, the customer and the customer's reaction to the experience.

In the experience, the business owner orchestrates a message of what is most important to the customer's heart and mind. Coming from the heart makes sense in life and in business. By creating attractive customer experiences, you are providing opportunities for a bonding response from the customer.

In Malcolm Gladwell's business bestseller, **"blink"** (Little, Brown), he provides some examples of how companies manipulate first impressions to appeal to the customer. Here is one:

Putting ice cream in a round, as opposed to a rectangular, container allows the company to charge more for the same product. We are willing to pay more for ice cream when it tastes better, and putting ice cream in a round container convinces us it tastes better….even though we are not conscious of our positive react to the round container.

Customers know unconsciously what a good product is; like good jam is Knott's Berry Farm. But if they are asked to stipulate why they think that, they come up with a plausible-sounding reason for why they might like or dislike something, and then adjust their true preference to be in line with that plausible-sounding reason. That is because our unconscious reactions come out of a locked room, and we can't look inside that room.

The brand is the experience.

Gone are the days of the geographically captive customer when merchants and service providers had the advantage of being the only place within driving distance. Today, even in cyberspace, the velvet-glove treatment is what your customers expect…or…they will shop elsewhere. Many companies today are shifting their resources to spend more devoted to creating a great customer experience.

In the 1980s, I had occasion to fly to Sweden a number of times on business and always selected one airline. Jan Carlzon, who was head of the Scandinavian Air System (SAS) in the 1980's, said "Each business experiences daily moments of truth...those brief moments that occur whenever a customer comes into contact with any aspect of the company and has an opportunity to form an impression." Carlzon's approach was exceptional customer service achieved by empowering the front line staff of SAS. The treatment I personally received from the SAS staff made me a loyal customer.

<u>Why your brand matters</u>

People categorize by brand. Your brand name needs to be within the top three of the category when the customer is ready to buy.

People will go with what they know and trust. Your business needs to leverage its established market presence by creating customer evangelists.

Let your customer win by establishing business processes that make it easy for the customer to be loyal to your brand. Provide the customer many choices to do business with you.

Continuously improve your branded goods and services to bring customers back again and again.

Ask the Coach: <u>How to Increase Your Sales</u>

Q: My business revenue was down from prior years. What can I do to increase my company's sales this year?

A: If you could do just one thing to help your prospective customers and your business, what would that be?

The answer to this question can only come from you. However, let me add a few thoughts to help you think deeply about your answer.

Consider giving more of what you have away. One of the most potent laws of influence is the <u>law of reciprocity</u>. The law is that people want to repay, in kind, what another person has given to them. Reciprocity flows from <u>the law of love</u> that is "the gift of giving" without the "hope of reward or pay," or serving others.

The law of reciprocity is not what can best be described as "transactional reciprocity." Wayne Baker, a University of Michigan professor and author of the book **'Achieving Success Through Social Capital'** (Jossey-Bass), says that, "Many people conceive of their business dealings as spot market exchanges-- value given for value received, period. Nothing more, nothing less. This tit-for-tat mode of operation can produce results, but it doesn't invoke the power of reciprocity and so fails to yield extraordinary success."

Baker explains, "The lesson is that we cannot pursue the power of reciprocity. When we try to invoke reciprocity directly, we lose sight of the reason for it: helping others. Paradoxically, it is in helping others without expecting reciprocity in return that we invoke the power of reciprocity. The path to reciprocity is indirect: reciprocity ensues from the social capital built by making contributions to others. And so those who help you may not be those you help. The help you receive may come from distant corners of your network."

Here are some ways to give more away in your business operations. If you are in a product business, you might consider giving out samples or providing test rides/demonstrations of what you sell to allow the person to get a feel for the product's value. If you are in the services business, consider providing a free sampling of your work or share a valuable insight (based upon your area of expertise) that helps the prospective client get to where they want to be. Even if the person who receives your gift never buys from you, she may repay your kindness by referring other people to you who want what you are selling.

I have found that people seldom call me when they want some knowledge I possess. But if they see me at a meeting or networking event, they will ask their question. By giving them the answer they seek, I have put the law of reciprocity into play. That is why it is important for service providers to attend networking events that their prospective customers normally attend.

If you hate networking, stop thinking about it as networking and just go there to share knowledge. By sharing knowledge with others, you earn trust, build your reputation and give or obtain resources. Information is energy but useless unless it flows around and combines with other knowledge in the minds of those you work and play with. So be sure knowledge sharing collaboration is a potent weapon of influence in your everyday activities.

Here are two self-coaching tips to exercise the law of reciprocity in your conversations:

1. Remind yourself that reciprocity is not about what you need but what the other person needs and how you can give that to them.
2. Frequently ask this question of others, "How can I be of help?"

Learn to speak from the heart by showing appreciation of the people you serve. Encourage others you work with to care by allowing them to observe your acts of caring. All businesses are ultimately people serving people and our life's work should come from the heart. Long after your products or services have been delivered, the feelings and knowledge shared during the business relationship remain.

Ask the Coach: **I'm not happy at work.**

Q: I am not happy at work and this is affecting my personal life. What can I do to improve my situation?

A: You are not alone. Many people are seeking to be happy. Even students at the university are attempting to discover, "What is happiness?"

 **One of the most popular courses at Harvard teaches <u>happiness</u>.** Positive Psychology, a class whose content resembles that of self-help books but is grounded in serious psychological research, has enrolled over 800 students, who learn about creating, as the course description puts it, "<u>a fulfilling and flourishing life</u>," courtesy of the booming new area of psychology that focuses on <u>what makes people feel good</u> rather than the pathologies that can make them feel miserable. "Positive Psych may be the one class at Harvard that every student needs to take," said Nancy Cheng, a junior majoring in biology.

After decades spent focusing on the psyche's dark side, now there's the emerging field of scientific research into what makes people happy. One happiness researcher attracting attention is Stanford's Brian Knutson. He is a professor of psychology and neuroscience who uses brain-image technology to measure satisfaction. Some of his research is designed to track how money affects the brain. In one study, he had subjects play a video game that involved, at certain points, the anticipation of winning money, and, at other points, actually taking possession of that money. He measured the difference in oxygen flow in the brain between those two activities. His conclusion: gearing up to do something can make you happier than actually doing it.

"Anticipation is totally underestimated," says Prof. Knutson, whose work is funded in part by the National Institute on Aging and the

MacArthur Foundation. "Why do slot machines have arms? You could just have a button--but the arm heightens the anticipation." 'I'll be happy when....' is the way many people think they are living their lives. Yet, happiness is not something that happens to you. Happiness is inside you now. You are motivated from within. You only have to allow happiness to surface.

Happiness is being aware, not only of the positive events that occur in your life but, that you yourself are the cause of these events--that you can create them, that you control their occurrence, and that you play a major role in the good things that happen to you. Happiness, said Benjamin Franklin, "is produced not so much by great pieces of good fortune that seldom happen as by the little advantages that occur every day."

Happiness isn't off in the future, but in living in the "now" and loving the moment of our daily experiences. We form an impression in every business or personal interaction. In the business world, we don't speak much about the heart. Yet, the purpose of doing our life's work should come from the heart---since all businesses are ultimately people serving people. We all need connection, belonging and meaningful contribution.

Viktor E. Frankl in "**The Will of Meaning**" states the paradox of happiness, "To the extent to which one makes happiness the objective of his motivation, he necessarily makes it the object of his attention. But precisely by so doing he loses sight of the reason for happiness, and happiness itself must fade away. Success and happiness must happen, the less one cares for them, the more they can."

The circumstances in life have little to do with the satisfaction we experience. Health, wealth, good looks and status have astonishingly little effect on what the researchers call "subjective well-being" according to "***The Science of Happiness***" by Geoffrey Cowley (with Anne Underwood) in Newsweek, September 16, 2002.

Psychologists have amassed a heap of data on what people who deem themselves happy have in common. Mood and temperament have a large genetic component. In a now famous 1996 study, University of Minnesota psychologists David Lykken and Auke Tellegen surveyed 732 pairs of identical twins and found them closely matched for adult happiness, regardless of whether they'd grown up together or apart. Such findings suggest that while we all experience ups and downs, our moods revolve around the emotional baselines or "set points" we're born with.

Ask the Coach: <u>Working from Home Tips</u>

Q: I'm in a business that requires me to work out of my home. What tips can you provide that will help me balance my work and family life?

A: There's a clear trend toward integrating work and home life as home businesses ramp up to full time operation and corporate managers are required to remotely work with employees in different countries and time zones.

The reasons driving working out of the home/telecommuting trend are diverse:

Many now work out of home offices integrated with their home life. Working from home has the advantage of eliminating commutes and staying close to family. In real estate terms, the presence of a "den/study" can add between 5 and 10% to the selling price of the house.

Family Dynamic Adjustments

The shift toward blending work and home is more of a psychological thing than it is making the home office space blend with the rest of the house. Working from home full-time requires family dynamic adjustments of who does what, where, when and how.

On a 24/7 basis, everyone must recognize the need to improve their own people skills and family communication in an environment where new furniture makes work look more like home.

Quickly Connecting Problem Solvers with Problems

The true structure any organization is not what is written down on an organizational chart, but what actually occurs as people connect through roles, influence and decision-making processes.

The connection and coordination necessary to get things done happens because of productive personal relationships based upon trust and reciprocity. Sharing knowledge and adding value to the organization depends upon the capabilities of workers to informally connect with others.

The challenge is to mine the tacit knowledge (in the heads of people where true knowledge resides) through providing an access method. The idea behind collaboration is that sharing knowledge leads to the co-creation of new actionable knowledge that leads solution development.

The key issue is getting people to think of themselves as part of a larger, collaborative community. However, changing people's behavior doesn't come easily, especially if they've been used to working independently in an office or factory location.

Understanding and facilitating business relationships, which flow through a web of professional networks and across functional boundaries and time zones, allows employees to create productive change. A company's ability to structure and control the process of securing productive relationships, face-to-face or via home-based telecommuting, will determine its success in the marketplace.

In today's "global network society" (versus your father's "local box society" where most people went to work in an office or factory box everyday), you can conduct business wherever there is a telephone, wireless or cable connection.

Within this interdependent global economy, our challenge is to develop inclusion and commitment in a world of telecommuting employees, "free agents" and even "volunteer" talent in different time zones and cultures.

Ask the Coach: Keeping up with Client Demands

Q: I'm an attorney who is having a difficult time keeping up with client demands. Having this much business is a good thing. Yet, I am spending too much time at the office and this is negatively affecting my personal life. I also seem to be getting less efficient in processing the work my clients bring to me. What can I do to improve my situation?

A: We live in a busy, complex and exciting world: where almost no one has enough time to act on personal choices. In today's 24/7 economy, we frequently feel rushed and impatient and can become easily distracted and forgetful from environmentally induced attention deficit disorder (A.D.D.). Dr. Edward M. Hallowell was the first to name adult attention deficit disorder or **adult A.D.D.** back in 1995 and now he is taking on the rest of modern life in his new book, **"CrazyBusy: Overstretched, Overbooked and About to Snap! Strategies for Coping in a World Gone A.D.D."** (Ballantine Books, 2006).

Technology and activity overload tend to be the consequences of living where everybody is trying to do more in less time. Yet, we must be able to maintain our focus and restore our energy as we bend, stretch and bounce around at work and in our personal life. We know that if we don't prioritize our life activities, we'll find ourselves spread so thin that we won't have time for those people and things that are important to us.

From what you have said, I can envision piles of papers stacked high on your desk and you hustling about trying to find where that client file is. For many professionals, these events are a daily occurrence. But they don't have to be. Experts say the act of getting organized is easy to put off because of seemingly more important tasks that require immediate attention.

In the April 21, 2006 issue of the **Michigan Lawyers Weekly,** Alita Marlowe, of Marlowe & Associates business and efficiency consultants in Southfield, MI, tells us the most common reason executives put off getting organized is it wasn't taught in school. "Procrastination and clutter is actually delayed decision making," she maintained. "<u>Time management skills</u> are also usually underdeveloped." Marlowe adds the biggest mistake professionals make is putting blame on a single person in the firm for the disorganization that "actually is the result of a faulty or nonexistent organizational system."

Marlowe recommended the first change that should be made is reducing distractions. "Each interruption costs 20 minutes of refocusing time plus the time of the original distraction." To drive home the point of just how costly inefficiency can be, Marlowe gave the example of a professional who bills $220 an hour. According to her calculations, if that person encounters six distractions per day at 30 minutes per distraction, there is $660 of lost productivity in one day, $3,300 in one week and $13,200 of lost productivity in one month. "Poor time management and disorganization costs at least $13,000 per month and causes lots of stress," she contended.

Stress, if allowed to build up over time, can lead to burnout in a work environment that doesn't engage and energize you. <u>Burnout</u> is a familiar term these days: it's the physical or emotional exhaustion that results from long-term stress or frustration. Chronic fatigue is a major symptom of burnout: one feels physically, emotionally and spiritually exhausted. Behaviorally, the burnout worker becomes cynical, indifferent and increasingly ineffective in the job.

According to Herbert J. Freudenberger, the New York psychologist who coined the term in 1972, burnout describes a specific condition. It is an emotional state characterized by an overwhelming and enduring feeling of exhaustion or aggravation. Burnout is a condition that develops gradually as the person's creativity and effectiveness erode into fatigue, skepticism and an inability to function productively. And when you are suffering from burnout, this can become contagious by having a profound affect on your coworkers and clients.

The bottom line is: Get some professional help to organize your workplace and reduce the hours spent there by becoming more productive. Use that reclaimed time to energize your personal life and create the work/life balance that allows a sense of well being to emerge.

Ask the Coach: Starting Over

Q: After over 20 years working for a global corporation, I accepted a buyout plan. Since I went to work right after college, I don't have an up-to-date resume and don't know what to be looking for in a new job. I have two high school kids that will be going to college soon and need to work supporting my family. What should I be doing to get back on my feet vocationally?

A: You are not alone. "Over-the-hill" in Corporate America is getting a lot younger. There are many more Americans turning 55 in recent years than turning 25. Many of the 78 million Baby Boomers, like you, are asking the question, "What am I going to do with the rest of my life?"

These later-in-life career changers don't care about taking it easier and often will work as hard or harder than they did in the jobs they left behind. A Merrill Lynch & Co. retirement survey of more than 3,000 Baby Boomers reported that 83 percent intend to keep working and 56 percent of them hope to do so in a new profession. Second careers are like second marriages---you are prepared to make better choices on what you want to do and whom you want to do it with.

More employers are recognizing that older adults bring skills and experiences to the table that can help the bottom line.

For example, in the world of consulting, "it can be a plus to have experience," says
Ms. Jackie Greaner, North American practice leader for talent management at Towers Watson. "There's not really a stigma about being older."

The same is true for other knowledge-worker jobs. For example, "the nuclear-power industry is an industry that is very hard to get people that are fully developed in terms of skill sets and capabilities," Ms. Greaner says. For employers, "it's very difficult to get that expertise."

Aon Hewitt's senior vice president for talent administration Ms. Erin Peterson says talented recruiters can be hard to find. "I find people who have a lot of life experience and professional experience make the best recruiters."

You should seriously consider taking stock of yourself and your life during this mid-course career correction before jumping into a new job or thinking about an early retirement. As Bernard Baruch once said, *"Age is only a number, a cipher for the records. A man can't retire his experience. He must use it. Experience achieves more with less energy and time."* Knowing who you are and <u>what you want to achieve in your second career</u> matters.

Thinking about a job search begins with knowing <u>who you are</u>, assessing your unique signature talents and understanding what you do best. Starting or buying your own business may be an option if you have the required skills, cash and attitude to make a go of it.

Even though you may have spent your career at a large company, your new search may lead you to small or medium-sized companies where less age discrimination and lower salaries exist. By identifying your transferable skills and packaging yourself for a new job function or new industry, you can greatly increase your chances of success.

For mature workers, the most common way to find a new job is by using one's social networks (51%) versus ads (12%), search firms (8%), mailing/direct approach (5%) and Internet (2%). However, don't make the mistake of networking too soon. If your goals are vague, the contacts you make can't help you much and your contacts may even be put off by your lack of direction.

Successful networkers never ask their network contacts for a job because they know that such a request generally doesn't produce the desired result. Just ask for an appointment with the avowed intention of seeking advice regarding how to advance your search or to seek new contacts. Such requests are harder to deny. If the person sitting across the table likes what she hears, she'll make a point of mentioning potential opportunities to you.

Here are some resume building and interviewing tips to keep you focused in your job-search makeover:

1. Narrow job goals to emphasize your strongest assets. Don't expect prospective employers will read your resume 5 or 6 times to figure out what you can and want to do. Have a focused direction--not a potpourri of "I can tolerate these other things, too."

2. Widen your list of potential employers. Don't let your personal perceptions limit your job-hunting success. Being uncomfortable with different industries or work roles can prevent you from getting to where you want to be.

3. Clarify and <u>polish your resume</u>. Highlight your most valuable and specific skills and competencies. Remember the summary is the most important part of the resume because most hiring managers only assess a resume for 10 seconds.

4. Hone your interviewing and follow-up tactics. Be sure to review your weaknesses, as well as your strengths, in both the interview and thank you letters to interviewers. By knowing who you are and what you do best, you will set yourself above most job hunters.

 Tom Rath: StrengthsFinder 2.0

 Marcus Buckingham: StandOut: The Groundbreaking New

Strengths Assessment from the
Leader of the Strengths Revolution

John G Agno: Women, Know Thyself: The most important knowledge is self-knowledge.

Wayne E. Baker: Achieving Success Through Social Capital: Tapping Hidden Resources in Your Personal and Business Networks

Ask the Coach: <u>Encore Careers</u>

Q: I have decided to take an early retirement package where I work and have a business concept in mind for a second career. However, I am concerned if my business idea can "make it" in this tough economy. Where do I go from here?

A: Once you know what you want to do with the rest of your life, it will be time to explore how to move forward into your encore career.

Today, many Baby Boomers are not simply delaying retirement, they are retiring retirement altogether by <u>starting new careers</u>. The fifty-five-year-old-and-up crowd is the only age group that is growing as a share of the workforce. More employers are recognizing that older adults bring skills and experiences to the table that can help the bottom line.

For years, the surge of nearly 80 million <u>Baby Boomers</u> into the second half of life has been described as a great gray wave, moving inexorably forward, building in size and momentum with every passing day. Boomers are likely to continue working, either part time or full time, as consultants or by setting up their own companies, surveys show. They want a "flexible" workplace that lets them take extended sabbaticals, then work intensely for shorter periods of time. They want to "phase-into" retirement by working fewer hours after 65 years of age.

In encore careers, most small business owners see their productivity and effectiveness, the ability to plan and the need to build skills in sales and marketing most important.

After working with entrepreneurs for several years, one major failing keeps surfacing -- too many have a fatal marketing "blind spot." These entrepreneurs thoroughly understand their technology. They may well be on their way to mastering the engineering and operational issues involved in delivering their product or service. Yet they persist -- often until it is too late -- in believing that the marketing issues are relatively simple -- **because everyone will surely love their new product or service as much as they do**.

Only after the product or service is "ready" -- or worse, after early sales attempts have bombed -- will they attempt to bridge the marketing gap. In my experience, this marketing "blind spot" is the single most common cause of startup failures -- in fact, I'm starting to believe, more common than all others combined.

That is why I recommend you test your business concept, on a confidential basis, with an experienced business consultant or mentor to get a feel for what it will take to build a sustainable business. Without having the experience of being listened to, engaging in brainstorming with and receiving encouragement from an independent expert, you are taking a huge risk in going it alone.

Yes, the global economy will be making a painful structural economic shift over the next decade. However, a recessionary period is an excellent time to build business because most prospective customers are ready, willing and able to abandon long-term business relationships, that are not working well, for ones that will allow them to do things quicker, better and cheaper. Also, information technology has improved small business productivity while making world markets accessible. Depending upon the product or service you plan to offer, many systems are in place to market globally, not just locally.

The most critical knowledge is self-knowledge. Understanding your unique capabilities and how to supplement them in building your new business is a good place to start while employed. Seeing ourselves clearly does many things:

• It allows us to control impulses and select the most appropriate behaviors.

• It shows us how to avoid reacting in negative and potentially self-limiting ways.

- Knowing our strengths and limitations makes us more understanding of others.

- Gaining an understanding of issues reduces conflict in us and in others.

Being aware of the affect of your personality and default behavior on people and future business decisions helps you to engineer a better communication and leadership style.

Spending a career as an employee has conditioned you to think as an employee rather than the self-employed. To move through this career transition will require you to exchange many of the assumptions and guiding principles that worked for you as an employee for those that work for a business owner. This will be vital in building a strong foundation from which to launch your new business.

Once you understand your personal capabilities and what you dislike doing, you will have a better handle on what you do best while off loading what you don't do well to others. There are a number of books to read as you move from being an employee to an entrepreneur. Here are a few: The E-Myth Revised, Strengths Finder 2.0, The On-Purpose Business, The Seven Habits of Highly Effective People, Can't Get Enough Leadership, and The Tipping Point.

Ask the Coach: <u>How to Improve Chances for Moving Up the Corporate Ladder.</u>

Q: I'm a woman executive with an information technology specialty in a large company. What can I do to improve my chances of moving up the corporate ladder?

A: Throughout our career, we continuously learn about our management style, how we lead others through interpersonal communication and how we cope with stress and other workplace challenges. <u>Becoming more self-aware</u> gives us great leverage in consciously exhibiting the type of behavior that gets us where we want to be.

Seeing ourselves clearly does many things: It allows us to control impulses and select the most appropriate behaviors. It shows us how to avoid reacting in negative and potentially self-limiting ways. Knowing our strengths and limitations makes us more understanding of others. Gaining an understanding of issues reduces conflict in us and at work.

 Our perceptions represent the way we see how the world works and they also strongly influence those we live and work with. Catalyst, a New York nonprofit research group, asked 296 executives of both genders to rate by percentage the effectiveness of female and male leaders on ten different leadership behaviors. Both genders said men are better at networking, influencing upward and delegating. "Women as well as men perceive women leaders as better at caretaker behaviors and men as better at take-charge behaviors," says Ilene Lang, president of Catalyst. "These are perceptions, not the reality."

 Three decades after droves of women started business careers, and at a time when fifty percent of all managers and professionals are female, women still comprise fewer than three percent of **Fortune 1,000** CEOs and just eight percent of Fortune 500 top earners. Women are severely underrepresented in leadership positions across industry sectors. The percentage of women Executive Officers and board directors in **Fortune 500** companies is stuck in the teens and single digits, while only about 26% of Senior Officers and

Managers are women. <u>The glass ceiling</u> remains unbroken.

A survey of women in high tech by Deloitte, the accounting firm, and pollster Roper Starch Worldwide reported that three of every five women in the information technology industry would choose another profession if they could, because of a perceived glass ceiling. Women, surveyed by Deloitte and Roper, say they're perceived as less knowledgeable and qualified than men. One woman surveyed says that women have a tough time "being taken seriously" in high tech.

Every corporate culture has ingrained biases where management attempts to maintain the status quo. This cultural immunity to change is especially difficult for women being denied promotions when the leaders of the company don't realize they are doing it.   If men don't think women belong in corporate leadership positions, they can create subtle male resistance in work environments where women find it difficult, if not impossible, to move up.

Since male executives have shaped the culture at most companies over time, women are at a disadvantage when it comes to gender-based differences in communication styles. A report, **"Women and Men in U.S. Corporate Leadership: Same Workplace, Different Realities?"** by Catalyst found that 81% of women said that "adopting a style with which male managers are comfortable" is an important or very important strategy to advance one's career.

Communication styles rooted in childhood training or unconscious beliefs can be tough to change.   A first step is becoming aware of how you talk at work. Here are some pitfalls that women especially can encounter in the workplace:

--using too many words to deliver serious messages
--downplaying your contributions
--using vague language
--phrasing statements as questions
--using an upward inflection at the end of statements, which indicates doubt.

Working with a mentor or <u>personal coach</u> can help you to be clear on the communication style at your level within the company and to confidently practice this style so you will be heard at work.

People who solve any serious challenge are the ones who change the way they think about themselves. <u>They convince themselves that they can change</u>, and they do change. Believing comes first, then change, not the other way around.

[John Agno: When Doing It All Won't Do: A Self-Coaching Guide for Career Women](#) (ebook at $9.99 and paperback Workbook Edition at $14.99)

[John Agno: Decoding the Executive Woman's Dress Code](#) (FREE)

Ask the Coach: Holiday Gifts?

Q: Our company has never given gifts to customers during the holiday season. Is this something we should be doing?

A: In another Ask the Coach, we responded to a question about how to increase a company's sales with another question: If you could do just one thing to help your customers and your business, what would that be? Our answer to both questions was to consider giving more of what you have away. One of the most potent laws of influence is the law of reciprocity (http://www.lawofreciprocity.com/).

The law is that people want to repay, in kind, what another person has given to them. Reciprocity flows from the law of love (www.LawofLove.com) that is "the gift of giving" without the "hope of reward or pay," or serving others. Remind yourself that reciprocity is not about what you need but what the other person needs and how you can give that to them.

Finding ways to make your gift stand out takes some thought about what would make the recipient happy.

Ask a Las Vegas cab driver, What's the best show in town? He will probably reply with something like this, "Oh, Jay Leno! My wife and I just went to see him. He gives a special show for taxi drivers at two in the morning. Otherwise, we could never afford to go. Kenny Rogers does the same thing when he's in town."

You wouldn't think that anyone as big in the entertainment field as Jay Leno and Kenny Rogers needs to give away their performances, but they do. Both realize that some of the best word-of-mouth advertising they could have would be taxi drivers raving about their shows. Why not consider giving something of value in your profession away to your company's best referral sources, too?

For your best customers, consider abandoning the usual baskets of fruit and cheese or imprinted coffee mugs at special times of the year. Also, avoid those silly end-of-the-year gifts of refrigerator magnet calendars given in mass by real estate and insurance agents. Many recipients would rather see the money you spend on calendars or fruit baskets go to a worthwhile cause.... like a charity or to help someone get to where they want to be.

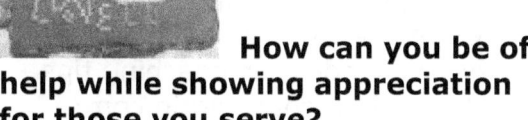 **How can you be of help while showing appreciation for those you serve?**

Determine who your best customers are (like the 20% who represent 80% of your revenues) and then send each a gift that keys into their interests or select a gift certificate that can be used to improve their personal or corporate capability.

Choose gift certificates of value, based upon the unique strengths of your business that can be passed on to others---for the personal development of an employee or to reward a key player. Such gift giving can be accomplished by both a product or service business that wishes to give more away in its business operations.

For example, in my coaching practice, I offer people the opportunity to sign up for free leadership coaching tips at: http://www.coachingtip.com/. The gift recipient receives periodic self-coaching insights in digestible bites for on-the-job application while fitting easily into his or her action-packed schedule. Research and self-coaching tip recipients tell me that people learn better, retain more and are positively motivated when supported by regular and frequent coaching.

All businesses are ultimately people serving people and our life's work should come from the heart. Long after your thoughtful gift has been delivered, the feelings and knowledge shared during the business relationship remain.

Gary Chapman in his book, **The Five Love Languages**, tells us that there are five ways people speak and understand emotional love. One of those is in receiving gifts: A gift is something you can hold in your hand and say "Look, he was thinking of me," or "She remembered me." The gift is a symbol of thought and the thought remains not only in the mind but is expressed in actually securing the gift and giving it as an expression of love.

Ask the Coach: New Year Resolutions

Q: It's New Year Resolution time again. Please give us some reasons why it is so hard to make our resolution goals.

A: First of all, we must understand that change hurts and that is why we all have a strong immunity to change.

Every year, we gain a clearer understanding that <u>without positive change, decline is inevitable</u>. The challenge is to recognize that what we are now doing can be reinvented by paying attention to our intentions. Yet, it is very hard to bring about significant change without changes in behavior.

Our emotional brain trumps our analytical brain

Given the high-energy cost of running the prefrontal cortex or analytical brain, the control center of the brain prefers to run off its emotional brain that has much larger storage capacity and sips, not gulps, fuel in the form of glucose or blood sugar. This part of the brain stores the hardwired memories and habits that dominate our daily lives.

"Most of the time the basal ganglia (the emotional brain's limbic system) are more or less running the show," says Jeffrey M. Schwartz, research psychiatrist at the School of Medicine at the University of California at Los Angeles. "It controls habit-based behavior that we don't have to think about doing."

The way to get past the analytical brain's defenses is to come to our own resolution regarding the concepts causing our analytical brain to bristle. These moments of <u>self-awareness</u> or insight (<u>in coaching</u>, we call them epiphanies) appear to be as soothing to the analytical brain as the unfamiliar is threatening.

Once you have had that initial insight or epiphany that change is necessary, you need to repeat the experience in order to reinforce it and to experience the potential pleasure that can be derived from it. The complex brain connections that are formed during the epiphany phase need to be supported to begin the process of hard-wiring the emotional brain.

"The epiphany is the catalyst and stimulus, but it's not the whole deal," says Michael Wakefield, senior enterprise associate at the Center for Creative Leadership. "You have pathways in place, and they're simply too strong to be changed in a single moment. You need to be able to integrate it into your psychological behavior for it to become part of a new pattern."

"Learning is the antidote to change resistance," says Wakefield.

"Learning lets you reframe the change from being something bad for you to something that can have value for you. You have to give people the sense that feeling uncomfortable is a normal part of change and address their concerns about losing face because of their lack of confidence and competence."

Here are five reasons why it is so difficult to achieve our New Year resolutions:

1. Powerful countervailing forces appear when we attempt to engineer positive change. We discover our competing commitments pull us in opposite directions causing us to spend a great deal of energy attempting to satisfy each: "I'm going to lose 20lbs but I really love to eat and drink." or "I am going to start a business of my own but I really like the security of the paycheck I get

from my job today."

2. Our overbooked lives and strong immunity to change try to keep us from relearning deeply ingrained habits. Today, 64% of people in the US say there is not enough time in the day to get things done. A poor night's sleep and tight work deadlines adversely affect our work performance. We turn on the TV to pass the time rather than moving forward to accomplish our good intentions.

3. Most people don't respect their strong immunity to change and, therefore, don't develop the support systems necessary to overcome this powerful and dynamic equilibrium to stay the same. However, there is untapped energy to be found if we can become less embedded in this immune system that protects us from change.

4. We don't give our brain enough time and energy to relearn deeply ingrained habits by developing and following a goal-achieving plan through personal determination, practice, repetition and the support of others.

5. Some feel they need a change but have a difficult time articulating/envisioning what that change looks like and how to plan to make it real. Developing the ability to respond to unpredictable change is very hard. Most are afraid to develop approaches to move from the more comfortable status quo. Learning to take risks by starting with small projects (where the impact of failure is not excessive) is a good approach to overcome this lack of initiative.

Self-directed learning helps you to discover an ideal vision of yourself to feel motivated in developing the abilities necessary to get you where you want to be. That is, <u>you see the person you want to be</u>---living with the capability necessary to create and sustain the new you. This personal makeover becomes the source of the energy required to work at the difficult and often frustrating process of change.

Now that you know where you want to be, the next step is to look in the mirror to discover where you really are today---how habits are making you act, how others view you and what comprises your deep assumptions and beliefs. Some of this reflection will represent gaps between where you are and where you want to be.

The realization of the gap prepares you for developing an agenda or plan of action needed for the detailed guidance on what new rituals to try each day to make the new habit sticky while you build your strengths and move closer to your ideal self.

We need more than <u>self-help books</u> to move forward.

Others help us see things we are missing, affirm whatever progress we have made, test our perceptions and let us know how we are doing. They provide the context for our practice of the new rituals. Although the model is called self-directed learning, without others involvement, lasting change can't occur.

Taking the personal initiative to generate innovative ideas and solutions to problems can require support in the form of <u>a personal coach</u> or a support group who guide us in handling important issues in our lives.

When we talk to others, in a safe environment, about the impending change, we reach clarity on what we must do to keep moving forward. Building our capability to accept and effectively handle change can release energy spent in worry and transform it into focused action.

Ask the Coach:
Transformational Leadership

Q: Is it a good idea to go outside the company for a new corporate leader?

A: Filling senior vacancies by looking outside for the best candidates can help to spark new ideas but grafting in new leaders has its risks. The cost of failure is high. Leadership transitions get riskier the higher up the organization they occur: two out of every five CEOs fail in the first 18 months (**Harvard Business Review**, January 2005). Corporate bankruptcies reveal that some CEOs fail on such a scale as to bring down the company with them.

Leaders in new positions often fail for a few common reasons: due to unclear or outsized expectations, a failure to build partnerships with key stakeholders, a failure to learn the company, industry or the job itself fast enough, a failure to determine the process for gaining commitments from direct reports and a failure to recognize and manage the impact of change on people.

When newly recruited, the following types of executives experienced the highest failure rates within the first 18 months: senior-level executives (39%), sales executives (30%), marketing executives (25%), and operations executives (23%).

Here are the major reasons for failure in the new job:

They fail to establish a cultural fit………………........................75%

They fail to build teamwork with staff and peers……............…52%

They are unclear about what their bosses expect…….............33%

They don't have the required internal political savvy….............25%

There's no process to assimilate executives into the firm…....22%

Yet, if companies don't seek fresh blood periodically, they can become dangerously insular, warns David Ulrich, professor at the University of

Michigan business school. "At fast-growing or fast-changing businesses," he adds, "you may find that existing managers can't scale up or transform what they do."

<u>Onboarding coaching</u> of the newly recruited or promoted executive can turnaround this high rate of failure. Onboarding coaching helps the executive more quickly adapt to the employer's culture, create rapport with his or her immediate team and find productive ways to achieve necessary goals.

Today, executive movements are increasing as companies make adjustments to become more globally competitive.

Focus on People

Leading a community, country or business transition through a cultural change is a tough assignment. Getting the people side right can make all the difference. Cultural transitions are times of heightened emotion where perceptions, feelings and hunches trump logic.

Everyone's decision making is emotional, not rational ... subconsciously under the control of their emotional brain (limbic system), not their analytical (neocortical) brain.

When people make decisions, their decisions are not just about rational data weighing of the pros and cons. Buying a car, choosing a mate, selecting a new home, following a career path, perceiving how the world works is all decided emotionally. Emotion is always operating below the surface and the executive doesn't recognize how important his or her feelings are at the time of the decision.

Today, many executives are driven by the fear of not surviving the transitional period and this fear can adversely affect their decision-making abilities. The turnaround won't be complete until the fear of failure is confronted in the minds of the executive survivors. Helping managers to become emotionally stable, free from the fear of failure, when making important decisions is the job of the leader.

Albert Einstein once said, "We should take care not to make the intellect our god; it has, of course, powerful muscles but no personality. It cannot lead; it can only serve."

Transformational leaders have a clear collective vision and manage to communicate it effectively to all employees. By acting as role models, they inspire employees to put the good of the organization above self-interest. They know and science has discovered emotionality's deeper purpose: the timeworn mechanisms of emotion allow two human beings to receive the contents of each other's minds. These leaders stimulate employees through the power of emotion to be more innovative by taking risks on-the-job.

Yet, after years of cost-cutting initiatives and growing job insecurity, most executives don't feel like putting themselves on the line. Add to that individual performance incentives, where a one-year term determines a large bonus, and investing in risky long-term payoffs takes a back seat. Most managers postpone risky decisions for fear of failure -- to not make incremental mistakes that can lead to innovative success.

That's why it is difficult to make the shift from a play-it-safe corporate culture to an innovation-driven culture.

Ask the Coach: How to Keep Good Employees

Q: My business has experienced high employee turnover over the last four or five years. What can I do to keep my good employees?

A: Your company is not alone. The ranks of the discontented are swelling. A Society of Human Resource Management (SHRM) survey found that 75% of the nation's employees are looking for a new job.

Due to dissatisfaction with opportunities, not being paid enough or burnout, employees begin looking for a new job. Low-performing companies have nearly twice as much turnover among top-performing employees as high-performing companies.

To become a high-performing company, you must recruit and keep top-performers.

Here are five lessons learned by employers of choice:

1. Employees leave their boss, not your company. The manager sets the tone and translates broad company policies so they make sense to individual employees. She must understand the strengths of each employee and work to fit people into roles where they can excel.

When employees know their boss cares about their opinions and helps them to understand and know themselves, their talents become recognized and applied so that each person brings his best to the workplace. When managers don't spend the time to develop a relationship with each subordinate, people leave. Having a mediocre manager, who has no idea of what an employee does and doesn't even try to understand, can be very destructive to a company.

2. Most people have learned not to listen to what management says but to pay attention only to what is going on around them on a day-to-day basis. The true structure of an organization is not what is written down on the organizational chart, but what actually occurs as people connect through roles, influence and decision-making processes. The connection and coordination necessary to get things done happens

because of productive personal relationships based upon trust and reciprocity.

Sharing knowledge and adding value to the organization depends upon the capabilities of workers to informally connect with others.

3. Is your company the best place for the best people to work?

Senior executives in the "Most Admired Companies" (surveyed annually by the Hay Group [haygroup.com] for FORTUNE magazine [fortune.com] believe in and use employee-based measurements to encourage cooperation and collaboration. And 40 percent of those companies chart retention, career development and other employee-oriented measurements. That's more than triple the percentage of companies that didn't make the list.

4. All employees have quitting moments when they entertain thoughts of leaving. Employees are more likely to leave because they want to do new things and take on more responsibility. Yet, employers frequently fail to create those challenges because they don't know the employee's capabilities.

One of the best ways to guard against employee disconnect is to implement a process of providing and receiving feedback to and from the employee.

Probably the most important factors in keeping talented people is to create a way for employees to feel excited by the work and to know that they are learning valuable skills. The quality of the boss/subordinate relationship helps employees get through those times when someone comes along with a new job offer.

5. Employers of choice know that ordinary people don't change that much, yet the power of a positive corporate culture can help them achieve extraordinary success. Their employees believe the company will treat them fairly, will consider their needs and interests, and will share financial success with them.

Employees know that hard work is part of the bargain of joining an employer of choice. But they also know they will not have to fight obstacles and insecurities alone because they will be surrounded with positive ideas and role models.

These loyal employees attract like-minded job candidates by telling others within their personal networks. Employers of choice leverage this attraction by providing employee referral incentive programs to reward employees for bringing other good people on board.

Ask the Coach: **Difficult Time Finding Talent**

Q: My business is struggling and I'm having a difficult time finding help. Locating real productive, energetic, creative and talented help has been very allusive. Any suggestions on where to turn to sort things out?

A: Many business owners fear their subordinates and clients will learn how inadequate they feel and are looking for help managing in a faster, cheaper, better global economy. Although hiding vulnerabilities is hardly new, this concern has been exacerbated by a new fear of either becoming obsolete or technology-driven toast in a world of business transformation.

"I've never seen business people have to fake it more," says B. Joseph White, past business school dean and interim president at the University of Michigan.

A good place to begin the search for help is to take a closer look at what has worked in the past and what has not. Once you have clear examples of good hires and bad hires, it would be important to look deeper to determine why one person worked out while the other did not. This deeper search should also focus inwardly to determine what affect you, as the business owner/manager, had on both the positive employee experience and the negative one. When we are open <u>to becoming more</u>

<u>self-aware</u>, the core problem may solve us rather than we have to solve it.

Developing commitment in a world of "free agents" is key to attracting talented people and realizing their potential. Many free agents and small business owners spend little time and money on their own professional and personal development. Yet, they have great interest in seeking positive change to improve their business development, career and financial and physical health. Within professional and business development, they are most interested in productivity & effectiveness, planning and sales/marketing. Producing results, attaining goals, achieving success and enhancing quality of life are important.

Reading business articles and self-help books is good. But, in my experience, there is no cookbook that has a recipe for your business-issue-of-the-day. And "going it alone" to struggle down one blind alley to the next is not a good use of your personal time and energy.

In this mobile employment age, it's rare to find a lifelong mentor available to support and guide you through your struggling business issues---but---work to get yourself an agenda-free surrogate mentor; Someone who has been where you are now, who will listen to you and brainstorm with you, provide an independent viewpoint, encourage you and who you can be accountable to.

Ask the Coach: <u>Dependable Part-Time Employees</u>

Q: I have a retail business and need dependable employees that are willing to work part-time during our busy times of the year and peak selling hours. Where do you suggest I look?

A: For a number of years now, many companies have been replacing full-time employees with part-time or temporary workers in an attempt to reduce operating costs.

But an increasing number of firms are having second thoughts about their employment policies and are actively recruiting permanent employees or giving contract employees de facto permanent status. Some enlightened companies are hiring or retaining older workers with flexible work schedules and ample training.

Driving this employment trend is an economic upturn and Baby Boomer retirements.

 In 2011, the oldest of the 77 million Baby Boomers began turning age 65---<u>the traditional retirement age</u>. Now 10,000 boomers reach the age of 65 everyday.

For years, the surge of nearly 80 million <u>Baby Boomers</u> into the second half of life has been described as a great gray wave, moving inexorably forward, building in size and momentum with every passing day.

Boomers are likely to continue working, either part time or full time, as consultants or by setting up their own companies, surveys show. They want a "flexible" workplace that lets them take extended sabbaticals, then work intensely for shorter periods of time. They want to "phase-into" retirement by working fewer hours after 65 years of age.

Why do Baby Boomers want to continue working?

Baby Boomers are becoming aware that they are experiencing a different type of retirement than the previous generation. Compared to other generations, these confident and independent Baby Boomers admit that:

+ They need more money than their parents' generation to live comfortably.

+ Their generation is more self-indulgent than their parents'.

+ They will be healthier and live longer.

Back in 2001, in a survey of boomers, 80 percent said they were planning to work past 65, at least part time, according to AARP. Many will do it because they have to; they need the money. This generation has every expectation that they will live longer than the previous one. Yet, few have saved enough money for 30 years of full retirement.

A survey of boomers by AARP found that two in five workers age 50-65 were interested in a gradual, "<u>phased retirement</u>" instead of an abrupt cessation of work---and nearly 80% of those said that availability of phased retirement programs at work would encourage them to keep working longer.

Working part-time is associated with better health and longevity. Work requires you to have social contact, use your mind and get some exercise. Doing something you enjoy during the best years of your life contributes to better mental health. And a paycheck can help you take better care of yourself.

A study by researchers at the University of Michigan and National Taiwan University found that just 100 hours per year of work is all it takes in a phased retirement; leaving plenty of time for leisurely pursuits. Looking at a representative sample of 4,860 U.S. residents born before 1924, the Michigan and Taiwan researchers compared those who worked 100 or more hours in 1998 with those who worked less. They concluded that by 2000, "those working for pay were only half as likely to have reported bad health and one-quarter as likely to have died" as nonworkers, says Ming-Ching Luoh, co-author and associate economics professor at National Taiwan University.

Why would you want to hire older workers?

In many companies, there is an assumption that older workers are much less capable than their younger counterparts and this belief has led to an unintended consequence of age discrimination. The Society of Human Resource Management (SHRM) says 59% of members surveyed don't actively recruit older workers and

65% don't do anything specific to retain them.

However, more Americans reaching their 60s and 70s are going to want to work, at least part-time. And research has shown that high-level work is getting easier for older people and keeps them mentally and physically fit. Fewer jobs require physical demanding tasks such as heavy lifting. A survey by SHRM found almost seven in ten (68 percent) organizations say they employ older workers who have retired. Baby Boomers, with more education than any previous generation in history, can be a good match for retailers who need capable employees working only at peak periods.

It is common today to find older workers on the sales floor at retailers like Home Depot and CVS and there is a growing presence of older workers in high-paying, high-productivity careers. Older workers have the skills and abilities to solve ill-defined business problems, like dealing with a difficult boss or customer, and many have a good work ethic.

John Agno: Boomer Retirement Life Tips (ebook formats $2.99)

Ask the Coach: How to Engage Employees

Q: My employees aren't performing well. Many seem to get easily frustrated, complain, waste time in trivial pursuits and become skeptical of other employees. What can I do to get employees more engaged in the work that needs to be done?

A: You are describing a dysfunctional work environment that could be headed toward employee burnout. Burnout is a familiar term these days: it's the physical or emotional exhaustion that results from long-term stress or frustration. Chronic fatigue is a major symptom of burnout: one feels physically, emotionally and spiritually exhausted. Behaviorally, the burnout worker becomes cynical, indifferent and increasingly ineffective in the job.

According to Herbert J. Freudenberger, the New York psychologist who coined the term in 1972, burnout describes a specific condition. It is an emotional state characterized by an overwhelming and enduring feeling of exhaustion or aggravation. Burnout is a condition that develops gradually as the person's creativity and effectiveness erode into fatigue, skepticism and an inability to function productively.

Traditionally, the worker is the one who gets the blame but research shows that the cause of burnout lies mainly in current economic trends, the use of technology and management philosophy within organizations. As managers become de-energized and lose confidence in themselves, these emotions are transferred to employees. Employee engagement and long-term improvements in corporate performance can't be accomplished with a burned out, low energy and low confidence leadership team.

Leaders can turnaround a failing work environment by helping employees move from the language of "blame" to the language of "personal responsibility." The first step is to instill confidence in the employee's ability to meet and overcome workplace challenges. Experience tells us that confidence precedes competence. A person must first believe they can succeed by developing a winning attitude reinforced by skill-building training.

As each person's unique signature talents are built into demonstrable strengths and then merged with other team members, a positive energy emerges. This energy force builds and reinforces each individual's confidence to create a critical mass within the team. This critical mass is often referred to as "momentum" or "being in the zone."

Here is an illustration of how this process works on the basketball floor and is easily transferred to the shop floor:

Basketball is an intricate, high-speed game filled with split-second, spontaneous decisions. But that spontaneity is possible only when everyone first engages in hours of highly repetitive and structured practice and agrees to play a carefully defined role on the court.

Great basketball coaches, military commanders and business leaders know that practice of the rules of engagement coupled with split-second decisions in execution by their team can make the difference between winning and losing.

Malcolm Gladwell, in his bestseller, **"blink"** (Little Brown), tells us that leaders know that if you can create the right framework (by everyone knowing the rules and practicing them), when it comes time to perform, your players will engage in fluid, effortless, spur-of-the-moment dialogue and action. <u>The leader provides the overall guidance</u> and intent to the team, coaches them in mastering tools and general techniques through practice and then allows them to use their own initiative and be innovative as they move forward.

Placing a lot of trust in your subordinates has an overwhelming advantage:

Allowing people to operate without having to explain themselves within the rules of engagement, focuses their energy and opens the possibility for extraordinary leaps of insight and instinct in decision-making. When the team is "in the flow," split-second decisions are unconscious flashes of insight that drive extraordinary performance on the basketball court, battlefield or shop floor.

It is the leader's job to keep the momentum going; so as not to lose the flow. Insight is not a light bulb that goes off inside our heads. It is a flickering candle that can easily be snuffed out by external means. Know that these kinds of fluid, intuitive, nonverbal experiences are vulnerable...and...your players/employees can drop out of the "zone" or "flow" when you, as the leader, start to become reflective about this rapid cognition process.

Confidence and energy are leading indicators of workplace performance. It is the leader's job to build confidence and participate in interactive conversations that pull people toward becoming comfortable with the language of personal responsibility and commitment.

Malcolm Gladwell: blink The power of thinking without thinking.

John Agno: Can't Get Enough Leadership: Self-Coaching Secrets

Ask the Coach: <u>Developing a Winning Attitude</u>

Q: With the football season going strong and the basketball season just around the corner, I was thinking about how I could transfer the "winning attitude" that sports teams have to my company team. Any suggestions?

A: We have mentioned that leaders improve their company by instilling confidence in each employee's ability to meet and overcome workplace challenges. Experience has taught us that confidence precedes competence. A person in the office or a player in a game must first believe he or she can succeed by developing a winning attitude reinforced by skill-building practice.

As each person's talents are built into strengths and then merged with others in the team, a positive energy emerges. This energy force builds and reinforces each individual's confidence to create a critical mass which is often referred to as "momentum" or "being in the zone." It is the coach's job to keep the momentum going; so as not to lose the positive energy flow.

Here is a checklist of ten questions to help you evaluate how well your firm is building a winning attitude and the practiced ability to succeed:

1. As the coach of your team, how much have you spent in the past year on personal development to improve your management and leadership skills?

2. List what time and money was spent per employee over the last year in training and development activities to build on workplace talents.
3. Does each manager have a good relationship with each direct report and know what that person needs to move to the next level in the firm?
4. Does each employee have a clear understanding of what they can to do to increase their value to the company?
5. In the last six months, has someone in the company talked to each employee about their progress in building skills and knowledge?
6. During the past year, how many employees believe they had an opportunity at work to learn and grow?
7. How many employees would say that their opinions at work count?

8. How many employees know the vision or purpose of the company? Of those who know, how many consider their job important in accomplishing this vision or purpose?
9. How many employees would say that they have a best friend at work?
10. Who would the employee go to with a suggestion, complaint or concern at work?

For your team, the best thing you can do is to demonstrate your leadership through one-on-one interpersonal relationships. You do this by participating in respectful conversations where you recognize your own feelings and those of others in building safe and trusting relationships.

Here are four guiding principles for one-on-one respectful

conversations:

1. It's OK to begin a conversation by confronting the other person with questions that seem awkward but set the stage for a respectful exchange. Why waste time on small talk? Just ask to-the-point information-seeking questions, like: "What are you here for? How do you want to spend our time together?"

2. Conversations are not meant to be structured. Be open to conversations that you are unprepared for and focused on the interests of the other person (not your purpose).

3. Don't get pulled into solving problems that may not matter to the other person.
Allow time for the person to get to what's really important. Provide spaces where people can express their doubts and fears by being a

thoughtful listener--without taking on the responsibility to fix or debate the issue. After all, you have invited the person to talk about what matters to her or him, not you, so allow time for the articulation of those thoughts and feelings.

4. Personal transformation happens when the right questions get asked--not by providing answers. When you focus on the solution, you are trying to sell the person something. When you allow people to answer their own questions, they discover what they were not aware of and what is needed to move forward.

Confidence and energy are leading indicators of workplace performance. <u>Effective coaching can happen on the dance floor of conversation</u>. You build employee confidence and energy through coaching conversations that pull people toward becoming comfortable with personal responsibility and commitment.

About the Author

JOHN G. AGNO is a seasoned corporate executive, entrepreneur, author and management consultant who today coaches senior executives and business owners to reach decision-making clarity by exploring unintended consequences of their future actions.

John helps you see things you are missing, affirms whatever progress you have made, tests your perceptions and lets you know how you are doing. His developmental coaching helps you focus your natural abilities in the right direction.

[Coach Agno](#) shares his decades of professional coaching and consulting knowledge to create a better life for many through [proprietary self-coaching guides](#); delivered to your smart phone, tablet, eReader, and computer or via low-cost paperback books.

Agno knows what caused the strain, stress and frustration of his successful clients in order to help them create effective and profitable solutions.

His purpose is to communicate these unique insights in blog postings and self-help books at prices so low that as many people as possible are able to afford and use them in their personal and professional lives. These powerful self-coaching solutions deliver life-changing possibilities for those willing to allow their perceptions to evolve.

What is professional coaching and how can it help you?

Download and listen to this MP3 recording of a recent interview of Coach John Agno for the answer to that question: http://view.vzaar.com/845767/download

To **Ask the Coach** a question, send an email message to: leadershipcoaching@gmail.com

If your question is too complex and you want to have a 50 minute telephone consultation for $299, send an email message requesting an appointment to: leadershipcoaching@gmail.com

Visit John's websites and blogs for more specific information:

www.CoachedtoSuccess.info

www.CoachedtoSuccess.com

www.SelfAssessmentCenter.com

www.ExecutiveCoaching.us.com

www.CareerWomenCoaching.com

www.LifeSignature.com

www.CoachingTip.com

www.SoBabyBoomer.com

www.Ask-Know-Do.com

For free leadership tips by Coach Agno via email, to subscribe: http://www.feedblitz.com/f?sub=644

Join us on Facebook: https://www.facebook.com/CoachedtoSuccess.info

Join me on Twitter: http://twitter.com/johnagno

www.ingramcontent.com/pod-product-compliance
Lightning Source LLC
Chambersburg PA
CBHW061506180526
45171CB00001B/63